Famous Lives

The Life of
Abraham Lincoln

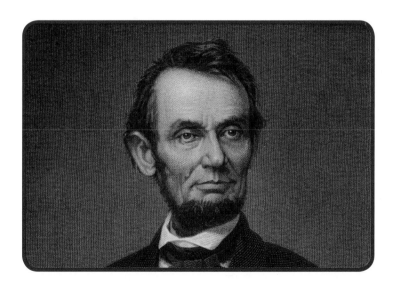

By Maria Nelson

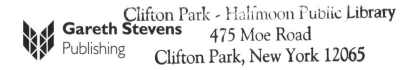 **Gareth Stevens** Publishing

Please visit our website, www.garethstevens.com. For a free color catalog of all our high-quality
books, call toll free 1-800-542-2595 or fax 1-877-542-2596.

Library of Congress Cataloging-in-Publication Data

Nelson, Maria.
The life of Abraham Lincoln / Maria Nelson.
    p. cm. — (Famous lives)
Includes index.
ISBN 978-1-4339-6343-8 (pbk.)
ISBN 978-1-4339-6344-5 (6-pack)
ISBN 978-1-4339-6341-4 (library binding)
1. Lincoln, Abraham, 1809-1865—Juvenile literature. 2. Presidents—United States—Biography—Juvenile
literature. I. Title.
E457.905.N45 2012
973.7092—dc23

[B] 4213   2011019787

First Edition

Published in 2012 by
Gareth Stevens Publishing
111 East 14th Street, Suite 349
New York, NY 10003

Designer: Daniel Hosek
Editor: Kristen Rajczak

Photo credits: Cover, pp. 1, 5, 21 Stock Montage/Getty Images; pp. 7, 13 George Eastman House/Getty
Images; p. 9 Hulton Archive/Stock Montage/Getty Images; p. 11 Buyenlarge/Getty Images; pp. 15, 17,
19 SuperStock/Masterfile.com.

Printed in the United States of America

CPSIA compliance information: Batch #CW12GS: For further information contact Gareth Stevens, New York, New York at 1-800-542-2595.

Contents

Boldface words appear in the glossary.

A Great Man

Abraham Lincoln was the 16th president of the United States. Many people say he was the greatest president! Lincoln was a very good speaker and leader. His actions helped free African Americans from **slavery**.

5

Growing Up

Lincoln was born in Kentucky on February 12, 1809. His family moved to Indiana in 1816 and to Illinois in 1830. Lincoln didn't go to school but learned to read and write. He studied law and became a lawyer.

Family

Lincoln married Mary Todd in 1842. They had four sons. Edward and William died very young. The others were named Robert and Thomas.

Leader

Lincoln was **elected** to the US **House of Representatives** in 1847. He ran for US Senate in 1858. He lost, but many people thought he was a good speaker.

The Election of 1860

Lincoln was elected US president in 1860. Before he took office, South Carolina **seceded** from the United States. More states followed. They were worried that Lincoln would outlaw slavery. These states formed the Confederate States of America.

Civil War

Lincoln wanted to keep the United States together. He was willing to go to war to do this. The American **Civil War** began in 1861. Then, Lincoln had to take a stand on slavery.

15

A Proclamation

On January 1, 1863, Lincoln said that all slaves living in Confederate states were free. Soon after, Lincoln gave his famous speech, the Gettysburg Address. He honored those who had died during the Civil War.

Reelected

In 1864, Lincoln was elected president again. He saw this as a chance to free all slaves. Slavery was outlawed in 1865. Lincoln then met with Confederate leaders. He wanted them to end the war and rejoin the United States.

Lincoln's Death

John Wilkes Booth shot Lincoln on April 14, 1865. Lincoln died on April 15, 5 days after the war ended. Abraham Lincoln's leadership brought a country together. He helped end slavery. Lincoln's memory will always be honored.

Timeline

1809——Abraham Lincoln is born.

1842——Lincoln marries Mary Todd.

1860——Lincoln becomes president.

1861——The Civil War begins.

1864——Lincoln is reelected.

1865——The Civil War ends. Lincoln dies April 15.

Glossary

civil war: a war between two groups within a country

elect: to choose for a position in a government

House of Representatives: one part of the US Congress. The Senate is the other part.

secede: to leave a country

slavery: the state of being "owned" by another person and forced to work without pay

For More Information

Books

Krensky, Stephen. *The Emancipation Proclamation*. New York, NY: Marshall Cavendish Benchmark, 2012.

Rosenberg, Aaron. *The Civil War*. New York, NY: Scholastic, Inc., 2011.

Websites

The Extraordinary Story of the Battle of Gettysburg
www.gettysburg.com/bog/bogstory/story1.htm
Find out more about the most famous battle of the Civil War.

National Geographic Kids: Abraham Lincoln
video.nationalgeographic.com/video/player/kids/history-kids/abraham-lincoln-kids.html
Watch a video and read about the life of Abraham Lincoln.

Publisher's note to educators and parents: Our editors have carefully reviewed these websites to ensure that they are suitable for students. Many websites change frequently, however, and we cannot guarantee that a site's future contents will continue to meet our high standards of quality and educational value. Be advised that students should be closely supervised whenever they access the Internet.

Index